Walking
the Path *of*
Prayer

Walking
the Path *of*
Prayer

10 Steps *to* Reaching
the Heart *of* God

Jack Hayford

Chosen

a division of Baker Publishing Group
Minneapolis, Minnesota

Previously published as part of *The Power and Blessing* by Victor Books in 1994; also appeared in the 2011 edition of *Living the Spirit-Formed Life* published by Regal Books

Published by Chosen Books
11400 Hampshire Avenue South
Bloomington, Minnesota 55438
www.chosenbooks.com

Chosen Books is a division of
Baker Publishing Group, Grand Rapids, Michigan

Printed in the United States of America

ISBN 978-0-8007-9915-1

Library of Congress Cataloging-in-Publication Control Number: 2018019479

Cover design by Emily Weigel

18 19 20 21 22 23 24   7 6 5 4 3 2 1

If man is man and God is God, to live without prayer is not merely an awful thing; it is an infinitely foolish thing.

Phillips Brooks
Episcopal Bishop of Massachusetts
1835–1893

Contents

Above and beneath It All

Walking the Path of Prayer

"In this manner, therefore, pray: Our Father in heaven, hallowed be Your name. Your kingdom come. Your will be done on earth as it is in heaven. Give us this day our daily bread. And forgive us our debts, as we forgive our debtors. And do not lead us into temptation, but deliver us from the evil one. For Yours is the kingdom and the power and the glory forever. Amen."

Matthew 6:9–13

The aged apostle Paul, as he concluded one of his letters, gave a series of concise commands summarizing essentials for disciples (see

1 Thessalonians 5:12–27). One of them was, "Pray without ceasing" (v. 17).

Whatever else may be said about living as a disciple of Jesus Christ, about walking with Him by faith and in love through trial and in power, clearly prayer is the one discipline above and beneath all others.

I have heard it said that more books have been written on the subject of prayer than on any other worthwhile theme occupying human inquiry or aspiration. Few thinking persons deny there is *something* to this practice. This has often been true even when the person denies there is someone there to whom prayer may be offered.

Prayer is a word and idea used by the materialist and the Eastern mystic to describe quiet creative reasoning or "transcendent" meditation. Still others characterize prayer as anything from describing a good feeling (toward a cause or person) to an impassioned cry for help from "whoever's out there."

At a fuller, deeper dimension for the disciple of Jesus, prayer is person-to-Person communication — a combination of worship, fellowship and intercession:

- *Worship* through adoration, praise and thanksgiving *to* God

10

- *Fellowship* through devotion, communion and conversation *with* God
- *Intercession* through supplication, fasting and spiritual warfare *before* God

"Praying always with all prayer and supplication in the Spirit" is a phrase inclusively covering this triad of prayer, one Paul enunciates in his concluding appeal to the Ephesians (6:18). The NIV reads "all *kinds* of prayers," a worthy translation that points us to a learning path of applied growth in understanding the *means* and *methods* of prayer.

The Bible's call to prayer is not a call to the mystical or the theoretical; rather, the pathway of prayer is preeminently learnable. It is not intended to be mysterious, but instead, always practical.

Starting with seven basic steps of prayer as outlined by Jesus when instructing His disciples *how* to pray, we will conclude with three keys to effective asking *in* prayer and attacking *through* prayer. Throughout we shall move toward applying the one constant the Bible teaches the earnest disciple: "Pray without ceasing."

To learn to live in the spirit of prayer is to learn to walk in the presence of Jesus. Always.

Wherever . . . thou shalt be, pray secretly within thyself. If thou shalt be far from a house of prayer, give not thyself trouble to seek for one, for thou thyself art a sanctuary designed for prayer. If thou shalt be in bed, or in any other place, pray there; thy temple is there.

St. Bernard
Abbot of Clairvaux
1091–1153

Confident Faith

You are all sons of light and sons of the day.
We are not of the night nor of darkness.

1 Thessalonians 5:5

Nothing is more crippling to effective prayer than not having confidence in our relationship with God. When Jesus refers to God as the Father, He helps us to understand the glorious relationship we are intended to have with Him.

"Our Father in Heaven"

"In this manner, therefore, pray: Our Father in heaven, hallowed be Your name" (Matthew 6:9).

Jesus opens His teaching on prayer with an emphasis on our relationship with God as our Father. In doing so, He establishes the foundational truth that we are given grounds for confidence in prayer on the strength of a Father-child relationship, which the Bible says is established and secured through Christ: "Now this is the confidence that we have in Him, that if we ask anything according to His will, He hears us. And if we know that He hears us, whatever we ask, we know that we have the petitions that we have asked of Him" (1 John 5:14–15).

Unfortunately, the concept of "father" has been marred for many through disappointing earthly relationships with parents or other authority figures. Because of this all-too-common human fact, Jesus made a point to show us the Father in a way no one else ever could. For in Christ Himself we see that God is a Father who transcends even the finest earthly father; He is able to redeem us from the broken images or painful memories of our lives. As we follow Christ's teachings about the Father and see how He showed us the Father in His life, we come to understand the power of His words to Philip: "He who has seen Me has seen the Father" (John 14:9).

The Story of the Prodigal Son

In Luke 15, Jesus uses the story of the prodigal son to paint a magnificent picture of what our Father God is really like. Here is a young man who wasted everything he had been given—his inheritance, his opportunities and his father's trust. He ended up working in a pigpen in a foreign land. But in unfolding this story, Jesus unveils God's heart toward each of us through five essential phrases. He shows that, regardless of what we have wasted, God's arms are still reaching toward us, openly and lovingly.

The first thing we learn about is God's *quest* for us. The father saw his prodigal son, who was still "a great way off" (v. 20). This shows us something unique and precious about the longing heart of God. As the father watched for his wayward son, so God's heart yearns and watches for each of us, even when we are far away from Him. In other words, regardless of what we have done or where we are, God loves us.

Second, we see that when the father saw the son heading home, he "had compassion, and ran and fell on his neck and kissed him" (v. 20)—he *received* his son. The verb tense used here to say he "embraced him and kissed him" (v. 20 NASB) is literally translated from the phrase "kissed him repeatedly." I have often reflected on this story, thinking about the reluctance the son must have felt as he drew closer and closer to home. He must have been uneasy about his return, feeling very unworthy. He had squandered his resources, wasted his entire inheritance and nearly lost his life. He had every reason to doubt that his father would take him back. But Jesus describes God's open heart toward us by showing how the young man's father welcomed him. The father cried, "My son was dead and is alive again; he was lost and is found" (v. 24). He must have received his wandering son with much the same joy that he had when he first embraced the son at his birth. It was as though his son was being born all over again. And in this same way, God receives us with joy.

Third, after this loving reception, the father called for the finest robe to be given to his son (see v. 22). The particular style of robe referred to was full length in cut—a garment reserved in those days for one who held a position of honor and prestige. So it is clear that this fallen son was being *restored* to his former position as an heir in the household. The privileges of relationship with his father were returned to him, even though he had lost the inheritance he had been given. Likewise, God not only receives us as forgiven sons and daughters, but He also restores us from the losses of our past. Although we may have abandoned the gifts He first gave us, He welcomes us back with a loving embrace and brings us again into our intended place in His will and purposes.

Fourth, the father had a signet ring put on his son's finger (see v. 22). How the hearts of those listening to this story for the first time must have leapt when Jesus related this part! They would have recognized instantly the significance of this action, for in ancient times the giving of such a ring indicated the son's full return to partnership with his father in the family's business. The ring gave him the right to exercise authority in all commercial or legal matters, for it represented the full weight of whatever authority or power that family's name carried. Thus, in calling us to pray to "our Father," Jesus shows that God invites us to let Him *authorize us as His partner*. Our prayer in the family name of Jesus is authoritative prayer. And that name is given to us freely and fully, carrying with it all the rights and privileges granted to members of God's eternal family.

Fifth, the father had shoes or sandals placed on his son's feet (see v. 22). These shoes were more than mere clothing. Old Testament imagery teaches that people in mourning had the custom of removing their shoes as a symbol of their sorrow or grief. By placing shoes on his son's feet, the father was making an announcement to his son: *The time of mourning and the days of separation are over! The time of rejoicing has come!* In this action we see the teaching of God's heart toward us: *God rejoices over us!* He rejoices at our return and at the restored relationship we share with Him (see Zephaniah 3:17).

Through the story of the prodigal son, Jesus illustrates our standing before God: We are welcomed to a place of confidence through the forgiveness given to us through Christ. Our Father offers us an authoritative right to be sons (see John 1:12), to function in partnership with Him and to extend His dominion over all the earth. No matter what we fight, whether the powers of hell or our own weaknesses, eventual victory will be ours.

This is what Jesus wants to teach us when He instructs us to pray, "Our Father in heaven." He is founding all prayer on a growing relationship with a loving God. And as the truth of God's reception and our restoration fills us, we will discover yet another benefit: We will learn to receive each other. We begin, with Christ's help, to see one another as brothers and sisters who have been received by a loving Father. And in that light, we cannot help but join together in harmony, lifting up a concert of powerful, effective prayer as people who have discovered God's love and who are learning to pray confidently in Him.

All who call on God in true faith, earnestly from the heart, will certainly be heard, and will receive what they have asked and desired, although not in the hour or in the measure, or the very thing which they ask; yet they will obtain something greater and more glorious than they had dared to ask.

Martin Luther
1483–1546

Transforming Faith

Be holy in all your conduct, because it is
written, "Be holy, for I am holy."

1 Peter 1:15–16

"Hallowed Be Your Name"

The frequently intoned phrase "hallowed be Your
name" (Matthew 6:9; Luke 11:2) literally means
"Holy be Your name" from the Greek verb *hagiazoō*,
which means to "make holy" or to "hallow." In
these words from the Lord's Prayer, we are invited
to experience the transforming power of prayer, as

Jesus introduces us to life's mightiest action: worship. "Holy be Your name" is a call to worship at the throne of God.

Realizing that the throne of God is an actual place will help us understand worship better. We are not offering our worship to some mysterious place "up there somewhere."

In Revelation 4:8, John describes his glorious vision of God's throne and the mighty angelic beings around it. An innumerable host is seen worshiping God, saying: "Holy, holy, holy, Lord God Almighty, who was and is and is to come!" And Jesus invites us to this place, not in an imaginary sense, but in a living, dynamic sense of worship. We are called to gather before our Father and to bring Him our own offerings of praise.

Psalm 22:3 helps explain why worship is so important and so potentially transforming of our life and circumstance. The text teaches that through their worship, God's people may literally make an earthly place for Him to be enthroned in the midst of them: "Yet You are holy, O You who are enthroned upon the praises of Israel" (NASB). Here we see that the dynamic objective of worship is not simply an exercise in religious forms; instead, worship is God's assigned way to bring His presence and power to His people.

In other words, just as we enter into God's presence with worship, so He responds by coming into our presence. Our worship invites Him to rule in our midst. When our hearts are opened wide in worship, God will respond. His presence and power will come to transform—to change us and our circumstances.

So we see a dual objective for worship: (1) to declare God's *transcendent* greatness and (2) to receive His *transforming* power in our lives, situations and needs.

In a dynamic sense, the expression "Holy be Your name" is both an exalting of God and a humbling of ourselves. When we use those words, we are inviting the Holy Spirit to make God's presence and Person real in our midst. Such encounters on a regular basis can only bring transformation—the conforming of our wills to God's and the shaping of our lives into His likeness: "But we all, with unveiled face, beholding as in a mirror the glory of the Lord, are being transformed into the same image from glory to glory, just as by the Spirit of the Lord" (2 Corinthians 3:18).

Worship by itself cannot bring about this transformation we need in order to respond to the Word, obey the Holy Spirit and walk in obedience daily; but worship *can* bring it about faster.

What Is Holiness?

To better understand transformation through worship, let's first examine the meaning of holiness, since that is the trait of God's nature that Jesus focuses on in this section of the Lord's Prayer.

As often as "holy" is used as a worship expression, it is too seldom understood. We tend to think of holiness as an external characteristic, such as a meditative expression, an organ-like tone of speech or a certain style of garment. This restrictive view causes many of us to feel intimidated or disqualified, because we feel we do not have the necessary external traits of holiness to earn God's pleasure.

Others consider holiness to be a stern, forbidding trait of God's nature, a sort of attitudinal barrier on God's part—an obstacle created by His flaunting His perfection in the face of our weaknesses and sins. This, too, is incorrect.

Simply stated, holiness is shown in the Bible as relating to God's *completeness*. That is, God's holiness acknowledges that He is complete; there is nothing lacking in His Person, and nothing needs to be added to make Him "enough." This meaning of holiness holds a promise: *Because* God's holiness is complete and because it is His nature to give, He wants to share His holiness with us to complete us.

His holiness, then, is not an obstacle to our acceptance but rather a resource for our completion and fulfillment as persons. God is ready to pour Himself into us, to complete those areas of our lives that are lacking, or unholy, because of our sin.

As we open ourselves through worship to this desired work of God, we will find His holiness and wholeness overtaking our unholiness. His personal power, in response to our worship, will begin to sweep away whatever residue remains from the destruction caused by our sinful past.

As we approach Him in worship-filled prayer, a spiritual genesis begins to take effect. The traits and characteristics born in us when we became part of God's family will begin to grow, making us more and more like Him. Just as surely as physical traits are transmitted to us by our earthly parents, so the nature and likeness of our heavenly Father will grow in us as we learn and grow in our worship of Him.

This truth is reflected in the command "Be holy, for I am holy" (Leviticus 11:45; 1 Peter 1:16), which holds a promise of holiness and completeness. This edict is not so much a demand that we stretch ourselves through self-produced devices of holiness as it is God's guarantee that His life in us will become increasingly evident and powerfully transforming.

So in teaching us the Lord's Prayer, Jesus calls us into the Father's presence to give the Father the opportunity to remake us in His likeness. That is transformation—a transformation that allows God to extend His Kingdom through us. And this personal dimension of transformation is only the beginning.

Beyond the power of worship-filled prayer to change *us*, it can also achieve a remarkable impact on *others*. In instructing us to enter the Father's presence with worship, Jesus points the way to a faith that can transform all our lives and the lives of those whom we encounter. He says, "Since God is your Father, let your worship in His presence make you more like Him; and as you do, His working in you will affect those around you."

Let's enter His presence with worship! Let's take the faith-filled step that moves us to experience the transforming power of God's rule in our lives and character through our faithful prayers.

So take a new stance. Move your posture in worship beyond one of passive reflection to one of power-filled potential for transformation. The Holy One we hallow in prayer is ready to invade every situation we address with His completing presence and power.

It is clear that he does not pray, who, far from uplifting himself to God, requires that God shall lower Himself to him, and who resorts to prayer not to stir the man in us to will what God wills, but only to persuade God to will what the man in us wills.

St. Thomas Aquinas
1225 (?)–1274

Responsible Faith

> Therefore, since we are receiving a kingdom
> which cannot be shaken, let us have grace,
> by which we may serve God acceptably with
> reverence and godly fear.
>
> Hebrews 12:28

"Your Kingdom Come"

The Lord's Prayer shows us how Christ intends us
to discharge our responsibility in prayer. "Your kingdom come. Your will be done on earth as it is in
heaven" (Matthew 6:10). Jesus' counsel on how to
pray illuminates a truth that we often ignore: People
need to invite God's rule and power into the affairs

of their lives through prayer. For if humans will not pray, God's rule in their circumstances is forfeited.

That thought runs counter to the common supposition that if God wants to do something, He will just do it. This sorry strain of fatalism infests most minds. But the idea of man as a pawn moved by the Almighty at His whim is *totally* removed from the truth revealed in Scripture.

"Your Will Be Done"

Jesus shows us that every human being is responsible for inviting God's rule—i.e., His benevolent purpose, presence and power—into this world. Rather than portraying men and women as hopeless, helpless victims of circumstance, the Bible declares that redeemed persons are hopeful and capable of expecting victory when they pray in faith. The grounds for this understanding can be found at the beginning of the Bible. There we find why Jesus teaches us to pray for the reinstatement of God's role on earth as in heaven.

Man's Loss

In Genesis 1, the Bible tells us that dominion over this planet was given to man by God Himself (see v. 28). This assignment was not only one of great privilege but also one that made mankind essentially responsible for what would happen on earth. Unless we understand this fact, we will never really understand that most of the confusion, agony and distress in our world today exists as a direct result of our having betrayed God's initial entrusting of earth to us. As a race, we have violated the responsibility God gave us.

This betrayal began at the fall of man. Through that tragedy we have suffered inestimable loss. Man not only lost his relationship with God, but he also lost his ability to rule responsibly. Man's ability and authority to administrate God's rule over the earth successfully is completely frustrated—whether the issue is environmental pollution or home and family management. And this lost capacity for a peaceful, healthful life has an added complication.

According to the Bible, "the whole world lies under the sway of the wicked one" (1 John 5:19). We not only betrayed our God-given trust of ruling the earth; we also lost to the devil the administration intended for us as humans (under God's rule). Since the Fall, we have not only been vulnerable to satanic deceptions, but by our own sin and rebellion, we have also contributed to the confused mess our world has become. Between man's sinning and Satan's hateful quest to obliterate, death and destruction have invaded every part of life as we know it—breaking relationships, dashing hopes and dreams . . . and ruining destinies.

God's Restoration

But when man's betrayal of God's trust turned this world over to the powers of death and hell, out of His great love, God provided us with hope: a living option in the Person of His Son. God sent Jesus, whose ministry announced the possibility of man's restoration to God's Kingdom: "Repent, for the kingdom of heaven is at hand," Jesus preached (Matthew 4:17). In that statement, Jesus made it clear that the rule of God was once again being made available to mankind. No longer did any member of the human race need to remain a hopeless victim of sin and hell.

In His ministry, both then and now, Jesus manifests every aspect of the Kingdom He offers. When Jesus heals, He shows what can happen when the rule of God enters a situation. When He answers need in any dimension, He is putting into action the power of God's rule available to our lives. As Jesus teaches, His objective is always to help straighten out our thinking ("repent"), to help us see what Father God is really like so we might respond correctly to Him and His Kingdom.

But at the same time that Jesus ministers, hell seeks to level its hostile devices against the Messiah and the Kingdom He offers. Consequently, Jesus demonstrates a warlike opposition to the invisible powers of darkness. He is well known for demonstrating God's love, but He is equally well known for the way He confronts the demonic powers of hell. In the climactic act of His crucifixion, Christ smashed these powers, making possible the offer of reentry into divine life with God and paving the way for us, His followers, to also strike down the satanic powers we encounter (see Colossians 2:15; Mark 16:17–20).

Man's Responsibility

In light of these truths, we must decide whether or not we will draw on the resources of Christ's triumph through the cross and live to advance God's Kingdom in this world. Participation in His Kingdom begins only after our acceptance of Christ (see John 3:3–5); we are then called to *advance* the Kingdom as we share the Gospel of Christ with the world around us (see Matthew 28:19; Acts 1:8). There is no more effective way to accelerate this advance than for believers to pray together.

Our first steps in faith are made on the feet of prayer, whether we are moving into victory or into witness. Our ongoing growth in prayer comes with recognizing that faith and victory are *not* achieved merely through the zeal of human programs but, instead, by prayer that acknowledges the triumph of Calvary as a release for God's presence and power.

This is why Jesus instructs us to pray, "Your kingdom come" (Matthew 6:10). With this prayer we are taking on our role as members of a race that once betrayed the King and forfeited His intended purposes to the adversary. But now He has endowed us, His redeemed sons and daughters, with restored Kingdom authority through prayer to welcome His entry into every need and pain of this planet.

The power is God's, but the privilege and responsibility to pray are ours. So let's hear and understand Jesus' words and come together at His throne, expecting and receiving the flow of the Holy Spirit's power! By His anointing we will find enablement to see God's purposes being accomplished through us and our prayers. This is what it means to pray, "Your kingdom come": to see the rule and power of the Kingdom of God as present and practical, to see the personal possibilities for prayer in every dimension of our daily lives.

"On Earth as It Is in Heaven"

May we never allow the promise of Christ's future Kingdom to keep us from possessing the dimensions of victory that God has for us *now*. Jesus is coming again to establish His Kingdom over all the earth. But that should not cause us to neglect our present prayer or ministry responsibilities for advancing the Kingdom as we share the Gospel.

Until He comes again, Jesus directed us to "occupy" (Luke 19:13 KJV). Our role as an occupational force entails drawing on the resources of God's Kingdom and power, reaching into the realm of the invisible through prayer and changing one circumstance after another.

"Your kingdom come. Your will be done on earth as it is in heaven." It is our privilege to pray this and our responsibility thereby to exercise the beginning of our reinstatement to partnership with God—to see the tangled affairs of this planet reversed from the fallen order to God's intended order.

He that seeks God in everything is sure to find God in everything. When we thus live wholly unto God, God is wholly ours, and we are then happy in all the happiness of God; for by uniting with Him in heart, and will, and spirit, we are united to all that He is and has in Himself. This is the purity and perfection of life that we pray for in the Lord's Prayer, that God's kingdom may come and His will be done in us, as it is in Heaven. And this we may be sure is not only necessary, but attainable by us, or our Saviour would not have made it a part of our daily prayer.

William Law
1686–1761

Dependent Faith

"It is written, 'Man shall not live by bread alone, but by every word that proceeds from the mouth of God.'"

Matthew 4:4

"Give Us This Day Our Daily Bread"

In Matthew 4:4, Jesus is talking about more than our having enough food or having our physical needs met. He is issuing an invitation for us, as children of God, to come to the Father daily for refreshing, renewal and nourishment for both our souls and our bodies. This phrase, "Give us this day our daily bread" (Matthew 6:11), registers a specific command for us to recognize our dependency on the Lord for *all* nourishment and to realize that this provision for our needs flows out of the discipline of daily prayer.

James 4:2 makes a strong statement regarding the necessity of prayer: "You do not have because you do not ask." The Lord is ready to release many things to us, but His readiness does not remove our place or need of asking. In other words, the promise of God's care for us does not bypass our need for prayerful, acknowledged dependence. The Lord Jesus teaches us to turn willingly to the Father and call out in prayer for Him to work in our lives. Rather than relying on our own strength (chin up, teeth clenched, saying, "I'm going to get this done"), we need to come to the Father in prayer—daily, dependently and gratefully.

Psalm 90:12 says, "Teach us to number our days, that we may gain a heart of wisdom." This is a sound-minded request for wisdom to recognize how *few* days we have and how much we need to employ them wisely. The psalmist also says, "My times are in Your hand; deliver me from the hand of my enemies" (Psalm 31:15). What wisdom! When we put our day in God's hands, any enemy we face can be conquered. Whether the enemy is ourselves— procrastination, sloth or other weaknesses—or the enemy is a demonic conspiracy Satan has plotted against us, *our Lord is able to deliver us*.

What Is Dependent Prayer?

Dependent prayer is not desperate or demeaning prayer. It is neither frantic (as though we only turned to God in a crisis, as a last resort) nor depersonalizing (as though God required us to grovel in order to escape His wrath). In contrast to these distorted views, dependent prayer is the *way* we gain a personal realization of God's unswerving commitment to us and *how* we participate in God's promised provision for us.

In the Lord's Prayer, the supplication "Give us this day" shows our need to learn an accountability for each day's hours and events, as surely as our need for having adequacy of food and other needs. Dependent prayer can help us do this. Jesus is not merely teaching us to request "bread" morning, noon and night. He is teaching us to ask for the Father's direction and provision in every event and during each hour of our day.

Committing each day's details to God in prayer—requesting today's bread—can deliver us from pointless pursuits and wasted time. Such prayer paves the way to victorious days.

"Daily bread" prayer is "daily victory" and "daily overcoming" prayer, because we are drawing on God's full provision for our sufficiency. He will help us to overcome anything that might wrench our lives from His purpose or cause valuable time to slip through our fingers.

Submit your day to the Lord and ask Him to provide for your needs. Whether your need is food or counsel for the day's activities, you will find that it *will* be provided. He will respond faithfully and abundantly as we set our times in His hands. And when you learn to pray this way, you will find another wonderful promise being fulfilled: "As your days, so shall your strength be" (Deuteronomy 33:25).

When we learn to pray, "Give us this day our daily bread," we find in the Lord a strength proportionate to each day's needs. Whatever challenges a day holds—confrontations, difficulties, even tragedies—we will receive the strength to face them. Just as we derive physical strength and nourishment from eating daily bread, so we will gain spiritual strength and nourishment when we learn the wisdom of acknowledging our dependency upon the Father—and pray His way.

Such is our dependence upon God that we are obliged not only to do everything for His sake, but also to seek from Him the very power. This happy necessity of having recourse to Him in all our wants, instead of being grievous to us, should be our greatest consolation. What a happiness [it is] that we are allowed to speak to Him with confidence; to open our hearts and hold familiar conversation with Him, by prayer! He Himself invites us to it.

François Fénelon
1651–1715

Releasing Faith

"Their sins and their lawless deeds I will remember no more."

Hebrews 10:17

"And Forgive Us Our Debts"

The next point in the Lord's Prayer addresses our
need for forgiveness. Some people use the word
trespasses, while most translations use the word
debts for this section of the prayer: "And forgive
us our debts, as we forgive our debtors" (Matthew
6:12). Both expressions are accurate and signifi-
cant. In fact, we need to pray both ways, for in these
two expressions we see the two sides of human dis-
obedience: sins of *commission* and sins of *omission*

(wrong things we have done and right things we have neglected to do).

"Forgive us our trespasses" speaks to our need of asking the Lord to forgive us for our having "stepped over the line." God is concerned about trespassing because He wants to keep us from the things that will damage or destroy us. In His Word He sets clear protective guidelines—territorial boundaries, if you will—that say, *Do not trespass here.* When we violate these commands intended to help us avoid that which is self-destructive, we are guilty of sins of commission.

On the other hand, "forgive us our debts" relates to our failures, to cases where it might be said that we owed it to the situation to do better than we did. But in failing to act rightly, we have become debtors. And such indebtedness can hang like a cloud over the soul, hindering our sense of freedom and faith for the future.

With this phrase of asking forgiveness, Christ fashions this dual dimension of release into our regular pattern of prayer: a request for release from both the shame of guilt and the pain of neglect.

But in order to grasp the power potential in this prayer for forgiveness, we need to see that both phrases—"forgive us our debts" and "as we forgive our debtors"—are conditionally linked.

Specifically, Jesus teaches that the degree of our forgiveness, our willingness to release others, establishes a standard of measurement. He gives back to us that measure of release and forgiveness that we show to others. And this fact brings us to the heart of life's most practical truth: *If I do not move in God's dimension of release and forgiveness toward others, I will inevitably become an obstruction to my own life, growth and fruitfulness.*

See it, dear one. Forgiving faith goes both ways: We must confess our own violations against God, and we must forgive others who we believe have violated us.

Forgiveness and Grace

Notice that by emphasizing our need for forgiveness of sin, Jesus is not shaking a stick of condemnation in our faces. The fact of our guilt is not the issue. The real problem is that we need to be taught to pray for forgiveness.

We are all people bent from God's original design and purpose. Not one of us is flawless; no one is without selfishness and pride. Sin is an inherited inclination in us all, and it needs to be forgiven. The call to pray this prayer is the promise that it will be answered. We need to pray, "Forgive me,

Father," and we need to pray it often. The Lord's Prayer, however, is not meant to level a focus on guilt but rather on grace.

Jesus taught us to pray for forgiveness on a regular basis, not to remind us of our sinfulness, but to keep us from becoming sloppy in our ideas about the grace of God. We often distort God's grace and give in to the deception that we can do anything we want as long as God's grace encompasses us. But in Romans 6:1–2, the apostle Paul demands pointedly, "What shall we say then? Shall we continue in sin that grace may abound? Certainly not! How shall we who died to sin live any longer in it?"

In calling us to pray, "Forgive us our trespasses," Jesus is not seeking to remind us of our failures; but He *does* want to sensitize us to sin and to the fact that sin hinders our growth in Him.

God's forgiveness is graciously offered and abundantly available. In the Scriptures He extends a warm invitation to us to receive pardon, cleansing and release: "As far as the east is from the west, so far has He removed our transgressions from us" (Psalm 103:12), "He will again have compassion on us, and will subdue our iniquities" (Micah 7:19), and "If we confess our sins, He is faithful and just to forgive us our sins and to cleanse us from all unrighteousness" (1 John 1:9). Forgiveness can be counted on. The condition, *confession*, is presented clearly, and the availability is promised: We can depend on Him to forgive us.

Forgiveness and Reconciliation

Jesus also describes forgiveness as being relayed *through* us to others. God's Word expands and applies the truth that we who have received forgiveness need to be forgiving.

Jesus directs us to go to anyone who has something against us and, in an attitude of humility and forgiveness, rectify our relationship with that person. And He says this must be done before we can make any serious, honest approach to Him in worship: "Therefore if you bring your gift to the altar, and there remember that your brother has something against you, leave your gift there before the altar, and go your way. First be reconciled to your brother, and then come and offer your gift" (Matthew 5:23–24). In Mark 11:25, He continues, "And whenever you stand praying, if you have anything against anyone, forgive him, that your Father in heaven may also forgive you your trespasses."

When we go to another for reconciliation, we must be certain we are not doing so in an attempt to justify ourselves. If someone has a difference of opinion or other problem with us, regardless of whose fault it is, God will not allow us to make any charge against that person. Christ desires that we be willing to go the extra mile and assume the role of reconciler—just as He did for us in reconciling us to the Father.

Understand that people often perceive a situation in opposite ways; this will help you to act as Christ commands. For example, if you have been offended, you may be completely unaware of the viewpoint of the person who has hurt you. To the other person, it will often seem as though *he* or *she* was the one violated and that *you* are at fault.

The effects of sin and Satan's discord in our lives makes us all terribly vulnerable to natural misunderstandings, and we need to learn this point of human understanding. We must acknowledge it in order to open up the reconciling process. Then, when we become willing to go to others (recognizing that their attitudes toward us are likely based on something they perceive as being our fault), when we accept the burden of the misunderstanding (as Jesus did to bring peace between God and man), *a real release will be realized*.

Let's learn to accept the responsibility for whatever dispute has breached our relationships with others. Restored relationships are possible when, in Christlike manner, we live out the meaning in this lesson: *Forgive me as I forgive others.*

Naturally, there may be times when the most loving, scriptural stand we can take is to confront others with their wrongdoing. Jesus did so, and the Holy Spirit will show us when we are to do so. But the spirit of forgiveness never does this in a self-defensive way; rather, it operates in a spirit of reconciliation.

This Kingdom order of forgiveness will not always be easy.

By nature we all prefer to be in the driver's seat, so to speak, and the ministry of reconciliation always puts us at the mercy of the *other person's* responses instead. But this is exactly where Jesus put Himself when He laid down His life to make forgiveness available to us. Though God has not called us to be someone's doormat, we *are* called to learn Christ's pathway to dominion. To do so is to see that this Kingdom path to power is in the spirit of the Lamb, never in one of self-defense.

There is no greater step upward in faith than the one we take when we learn to forgive—and *do it.* Forgiveness blesses people who need our love and acceptance, and it releases us to bright horizons of joy, health and dynamic faith in prayer.

It has been well said that no man ever sank under the burden of the day. It is when tomorrow's burden is added to the burden of today that the weight is more than a man can bear. Never load yourselves so, my friends. If you find yourselves so loaded, at least remember this: it is your own doing, not God's. He begs you to leave the future to Him and mind the present.

George MacDonald
1824–1905

Obedient Faith

The Lord knows how to deliver the godly
out of temptations and to reserve the unjust
under punishment for the day of judgment.

2 Peter 2:9

"And Do Not Lead Us into Temptation"

Our next step brings us to the most paradoxical
part of the Lord's Prayer: "And do not lead us
into temptation, but deliver us from the evil one"
(Matthew 6:13). At first these words seem a bit
confusing in light of other Scriptures that assure
us God does not tempt anyone. James 1:13–14
makes this clear: God tempts no man, but when

we are tempted, we are drawn away of our own lusts and enticed.

We know, then, that in teaching us to pray, "Lead us not into temptation," Jesus does not teach us that we must beg God not to trick us into sinning. Nor does Jesus teach us a prayer for escaping the demands of growth that come through God's leading us—and He *does* lead us—into trials.

To understand what Jesus *does* teach, we must first gain a clear understanding of the word *temptation*, a word that carries a two-sided meaning. First, temptation essentially has to do with the desire of an adversary to test and break through our defenses. Second, temptation deals with the strength gained through encountering an adversary; that is, when the one who is tested overcomes the test, the resulting victory builds strength. Temptation, therefore, is both positive and negative, depending on our viewpoint and response.

In that light, Jesus does not suggest that we should ask or expect to avoid the kind of confrontation He faced with Satan. In fact, the Bible tells us that the Holy Spirit *led* Christ into that experience of conflict with the devil (see Matthew 4:1). As a direct result of overcoming this time of temptation, Jesus declared victory and dominion over the enemy (see John 14:30). So, clearly, this section of the Lord's Prayer holds a promise of victory, rather than a plea for relief from struggle.

With these words, "lead us not," we come to the Lord in advance and commit ourselves to receive His deliverances rather than allow temptation to entangle us in its snares. This prayer does not question God's nature or leading—it declares we are casting ourselves on Him.

We do not ask God, *Please don't play with us as pawns on a chess board, risking our loss by leading us into questionable situations.* Instead, when we examine various translations of this challenging verse and note the tense and mood of the Greek verb translated "lead" or "bring unto," we discover that the phrase "lead us not into temptation" is a guarantee of victory—if we will take it!

"But Deliver Us from the Evil One"

Jesus' prayer lesson teaches us the need to establish our steps in advance through regular prayer in order to resist the evil one (see James 4:7). A clear translation of Matthew 6:13 shows that Jesus actually directs us to pray, *Father, should we at any point be led into any temptation, test or trial, we want to come out delivered and victorious.*

So the issue in this portion of the Lord's Prayer is a questioning not of God's character but, rather, *ours.* Such a prayer says: *Lord, You won't lead or introduce me into any situations but those for my refinement, growth and victory. When I encounter circumstances designed to lead me astray, therefore, I will recognize that it is not Your will for me to walk that way. God, I am committing myself in advance to want victory, to seek deliverance and to take the way of escape You have promised me.*

Because we are so easily deluded by temptation, we must understand the intent of Jesus' prayer. Once again, He is not suggesting it is God's nature to trick or corrupt us by tempting us. In fact, He is emphasizing it is God's nature to "deliver us from evil." The prayer simply establishes a commitment on our part to receive the triumphant life Christ offers us in dominion over evil. Our lives become more effective when we avoid being neutralized by hell's manipulations or by our flesh's cry for self-indulgence.

Paul wrote, "And the Lord will deliver me from every evil work and preserve me for His heavenly kingdom. To Him be glory forever and ever. Amen!" (2 Timothy 4:18). He also wrote, "No temptation has overtaken you except such as is common to man; but God is faithful, who will not allow you to be tempted beyond what you are able, but with the temptation will also make the way of escape, that you may be able to bear it" (1 Corinthians 10:13). Here, then, is obedient faith confronting the reality of our vulnerability to temptation, which is sometimes quick in its rise and subtle in its approach.

The prayer "deliver us from the evil one" does not remove temptation's challenge, but it does help us understand that we are not evil simply because we are tempted. Furthermore, we have a certain promise: God has a doorway of exit for us. When temptation comes, asking Him to "deliver us from evil" ensures us a way out.

What a great certainty this is! What a beautiful climax to this lesson in the Lord's Prayer! If we seek Him, God *will* deliver us out of temptation. Thus, when we pray, "Deliver us from evil," we are committing ourselves to walk in triumph and dominion over the things that would seek to conquer us—to live in obedient faith. And to live this way is to count on God's deliverance, for He is able (see Hebrews 2:18).

We will do better in dealing with temptations if we keep an eye on them in the very beginning. Temptations are more easily overcome if they are never allowed to enter our minds. Meet them at the door as soon as they knock, and do not let them in.

Thomas à Kempis
1380–1471

Trusting Faith

> Therefore humble yourselves under the mighty hand of God, that He may exalt you in due time.
>
> 1 Peter 5:6

"For Yours Is the Kingdom"

Our study of the Lord's Prayer concludes with these words of trusting faith: "For Yours is the kingdom and the power and the glory forever" (Matthew 6:13). Here is the active expression of a heart that has absolute assurance of the complete triumph of God—in *His* time.

Turn with me to Acts 1:6–7. I think the words of Jesus to His disciples will give us additional insight into this section of the Lord's Prayer: "Therefore, when they had come together, they asked Him, saying, 'Lord, will You at this time restore the kingdom to Israel?' And He said to them, 'It is not for you to know times or seasons which the Father has put in His own authority.'" Jesus spoke these words following His resurrection, as He was giving final instructions to His disciples before His ascension. He had been explaining principles of the Kingdom of God (see vv. 3–5).

In light of what He was teaching and with the facts of His crucifixion and resurrection behind them, Jesus' disciples wondered, *Just when will this kingdom finally come?* They probably felt sure that the time *must* be ripe for the Messianic Kingdom to be established. Surely now was the time for Israel to be liberated from Roman oppression.

But Jesus patiently replied that it was not for them to know when His Kingdom would be established (see v. 7). He was not stalling them. Nor was He denying the ultimate establishment of His Kingdom someday. But He was redirecting their understanding.

The issue of the Kingdom's coming with power is asserted in His very next words: "But you shall receive power when the Holy Spirit has come upon you; and you shall be witnesses to Me in Jerusalem, and in all Judea and Samaria, and to the end of the earth" (Acts 1:8). He was showing them the Holy Spirit's coming was a mission to work the *spread* of the Kingdom *through* them, not the *completion* of the Kingdom *for* them.

This conversation between Jesus and His disciples, with Jesus' promise of the Holy Spirit's power in relation to the timing of His Kingdom, can help us understand the meaning of the concluding phrase of the Lord's Prayer. We can see that Jesus was teaching the pathway to trust—to the knowledge that when we have prayed in faith, we can rest firm in our confidence God has heard. He *will* attend to all issues; and even when we do not see *our* timing in the answer, *His* purposes are not being lost.

Consider the words, "Yours is the kingdom" (Matthew 6:13).

For many, these words seem to point to the future. But Jesus taught very clearly that in certain respects the presence and power of His Kingdom are given to us *now*: "Do not fear, little flock, for it is your Father's good pleasure to give you the kingdom" (Luke 12:32). Although we will only experience the fullest expression of His Kingdom when

He comes again, we must not diminish the fact that this prayer is dealing with God's rule and power impacting situations *now*. Wherever the Spirit is given room and allowed to work, the Kingdom "comes."

So here, at prayer, Jesus reminds us that such privileged participation in the power of His Kingdom life has terms: We are called to submit to God's rule in our lives (see 1 Peter 5:6).

"And the Power and the Glory Forever"

The first factor in developing a trusting faith is learning that the rule, the power and the glory are God's. He allows us to share with Him, but He is Lord. He gives us power, but only He is omnipotent. He teaches us, but He alone is all-knowing. And submission and humility are prerequisites to sharing God's authority. Satan flees the believer who has learned the truth of "Yours is the power" (see James 4:7).

Faith is ever and always challenging the status quo where evil reigns, where pain and sickness prevail, where hatred and hellishness rule or where human failure breeds confusion. As we learn to live under the Holy Spirit's rule, we will be able to take a bold, confrontive stance against all in opposition to that rule whether of demonic, fleshly or earthly nature. Such a stance says, *I rely upon the One who claims ultimate and final rule everywhere. I won't give way to any lie that attempts to cast doubt on God's ultimate, complete victory.* And when we do this, we will often see results that would not have been realized without Kingdom praying.

But what about when we do not see any results? What then? The disciples' inquiry echoes from our lips too: Will the Kingdom be now?

In answer to this question, Jesus teaches us to pray, "Yours is the kingdom" in Matthew 6:13. He is leading us to realize that even though answers may not yet fully appear, two things come from trusting faith: (1) the knowledge that the ultimate triumph of God's manifest power shall come in His time and (2) the assurance that until that time, He has given us His Spirit to enable us to do His will.

Here is our fortress of confidence. Though time may pass without our seeing "victory" as we would interpret it, we know—and pray with praise—that we have not been deserted. God's Holy Spirit brings us His presence and power right now, for whatever circumstances we encounter.

There will be times when we will see God's Kingdom power in action—with healings and miracles—in our lives. But there will also be times the Lord simply says, *Trust Me—the time is not yet,*

*but in the meantime, the power of My Spirit will
sustain you.*

Great power and privilege are given to the
Church. "Nothing will be impossible for you,"
Jesus says (Matthew 17:20). Yet, as certain as the
promise and possibilities are, we must humbly and
honestly acknowledge there are times when we
seem unable to *possess* the promise. Such acknowl-
edgments are not statements of doubt. Nor are
they cases of God's refusing to grant us an answer
or fulfill His Word.

God's promises are true, and His Word is faithful.
But the Kingdom timing is His too! And so are the
ultimate power and glory.

When we conclude the Lord's Prayer with,
"Yours is the kingdom and the power and the glory,"
we are not being either passive or merely poetic. We
are reflecting the power of trusting faith—faith that
stands in firm confidence, regardless of circumstances. Such faith declares, *Lord, to You belongs
all Kingdom authority, for You are the possessor of
all! And as I gain that Kingdom, a portion at a time,
I trust You—for the Kingdom is Yours.*

There are no greater grounds for rest and con-
tentment in life than the certainty wrapped in these
words:

"Yours is the kingdom"—all rule *belongs* to God.

"Yours is the power"—all mightiness *flows* from Him.

"Yours is the glory"—His victory *shall be* complete.

With this kind of prayer comes boldness, confidence and rest. For when all is said and done, our greatest resource is to rest in God's greatness. In Him we find confidence that our every need will be met, our ultimate victory realized and—in His time, by His purpose and for His glory—all things will resolve unto His wisest, richest and best.

So let's join, now and ever, the angelic throng around His throne, uniting our concert of prayer and praise with theirs, saying:

> "Holy, holy, holy,
> Lord God *Almighty*,
> Who was and is and is to come!"
>
> Revelation 4:8,
> emphasis added

Even if all the things that people prayed for happened, which they do not, this would not prove what Christians mean by the efficacy of prayer. For prayer is request. The essence of request, as distinct from compulsion, is that it may or may not be granted. And if an infinitely wise Being listens to the requests of finite and foolish creatures, of course He will sometimes grant and sometimes refuse them. Invariable "success" in prayer would not prove the Christian doctrine at all. It would prove something more like magic—a power in certain human beings to control, or compel, the course of nature.

C. S. Lewis
1898–1963

Jesus' Lessons on Bold Faith

Let us therefore come boldly to the throne
of grace, that we may obtain mercy and find
grace to help in time of need.

Hebrews 4:16

As is my usual habit, I awoke early for the purpose of prayer. But when I sat on the edge of
the bed, I heard a whisper to my heart: *You have
forgotten the discipline of daily devotional habit.*

I knew immediately what the Holy Spirit was
dealing with me about. And though the prompting
to some might have seemed a rebuke, I did not pro-
test because I understood He was speaking to me
about my personal walk with Jesus. The issue was

being *quiet* and *with* Him as compared to passionately praying about issues and asking for answers. There is a difference.

It was as though God was saying, *I am not just looking, Jack, for your petitions and powerful, passionate prayers. I will honor your seeking to see My Kingdom enter the world, as you pray for the invasion of My power into hell's darkness. And I do welcome your worship as you extol My name. But Child, I wish you would simply spend more time with Me—to know My heart and let Me deal with yours, to give you instructions in the personal matters of your private life as you learn to wait on Me.*

Now, I had not been totally closed off to simply being in the Lord's presence. But I had become so excited, indeed zealous, in the application of great principles of supplication, intercession and faith's confession (things I'd begun to learn and practice) that the *power* potential in prayer was distracting me from the *devotional* aspect of a personal walk with Jesus. But at that moment, the Lord was reminding me of His desire for *me*: *I just want you to be with Me.*

A Daily Devotional Habit

Daybreak is a booklet I wrote following that encounter, a handbook outlining details for a daily devotional habit. It points to a more personal and intimate walk with the Lord, one in which we bring our days to Him, to allow Him to order our steps. As a result, we learn to function in the wisdom of daily devotions in the presence of Jesus. All prayer is best cultivated on the foundation of a quiet time. During regular quiet times with the Savior, relationship becomes deepened and established in a personal dimension.

By reason of that small book's abundant availability and inexpensive price, I will not elaborate the patterns for my daily devotional habit here. Instead, the following outline from the book provides a simple structure to prompt your private, personal walk with Jesus—your "talk time" with the Savior:

I. *Enter His Presence*

Begin by presenting yourself with thanksgiving and praise, placing your whole being before God (see Mark 12:30).

A. Find a new reason every day to do this (see Psalms 100:4; 118:24).

B. Present your body in worship to Him (see Psalm 63:3–4; Romans 12:1).

C. Sing a new song to the Lord (see Psalm 96:1–2; Colossians 3:16).

D. Allow the Holy Spirit to assist your praise (see 1 Corinthians 14:15; Jude 1:20).

II. *Open Your Heart*

Present your heart to God with confession for cleansing, diligently seeking purity (see Proverbs 4:23).

A. Invite the Lord to search your heart (see Psalm 139:23–24).

B. Recognize the danger of deception (see Jeremiah 17:9; 1 John 1:6–10).

C. Set a monitor on your mouth and heart (see Psalms 19:14; 49:3).

D. Keep Christ's purposes and goals in view (see Psalm 90:12; Philippians 3:13–14).

III. *Order Your Day*

In obedience to our Lord, present your day and submit to His ways and rule in your life (see 1 Peter 5:6–11).

A. Surrender your day to God (see Deuteronomy 33:25; Psalms 31:14–15; 37:4–5).

B. Indicate your dependence on Him (see Psalm 131:1–3; Proverbs 3:5–7).

    C. Request specific direction for today (see Psalm 25:4–5; Isaiah 30:21).

    D. Obey Jesus' explicit instructions (see Matthew 6:11; 7:7–8).

Taking these simple pointers, allow yourself regular times to be "up and early with the Lord." Never let the adversary condemn you because you miss one or more days. Let every time you *are* with the Savior be as precious to you as He wants it to be.

You will find that early-morning hours are usually best to find unbroken, undisturbed occasions for quiet in His presence. Jesus' pattern was to pray alone before daylight, which deserves emulation (see Mark 1:35). And remember, use the above outline for a guideline, not a regimented requirement. I have found it helps to target Him (His presence), my heart (and purity) and my days (His counsel about the details of my life).

In the environment of this kind of walk with Christ, boldness of faith and expanding intercessory prayer will grow. Our petitions, however simple or complex, will become confident requests when we simply come to know Jesus. So with this resource in hand and intimacy as our priority, the beginning of a prayer discipline is in place.

Perseverance in Prayer

Moving forward from this foundation, a disciple's growth in prayer will broaden in its dimensions. Ephesians 6:18 tells us to pray "always with all prayer and supplication in the Spirit, being watchful to this end with all perseverance and supplication." In this text, the Greek word *proskarterēsis* ("perseverance") means steadfastness and constancy in prayer.

The idea is clear and should be readily understood. But the concept of perseverance is still often twisted in some people's thinking to mean something other than keeping at it. Because of the importance of the idea presented here and because of the false images surrounding a key word to understanding this passage, let's study the matter of perseverance.

Some mistakenly view persevering in prayer as a gutsy, grit-your-teeth, "I'll hang tough till God finally hears me and does something" kind of exercise. Misunderstanding perseverance and persistence can also breed a sense that it is a complaint about our state of affairs: *God, I've been praying for a long time. Can't You see where things are? I need help, I need it now, and I am tired of waiting!* One view supposes *earning* an answer; the other supposes we can or ought to "bully" God. But heaven really does not need this exhortation from us. God is never passive.

Yet the idea has somehow evolved that perseverance in prayer is needed in order either to gain God's approval or somehow to win His interest. Curiously, two of Jesus' parables have been used to support this distorted idea. Both have been used to preach persistence, or perseverance, in prayer, but to draw that idea from these stories is to violate the text. The lessons intended by Jesus are to beget *boldness* and *assurance* when we pray—to ask freely and expect greatly.

Asking for Bread at Midnight

In Luke 11:5–8, Jesus follows up His teaching on the Lord's Prayer by explaining the liberty one has in seeking help from a friend:

> "Which of you shall have a friend, and go to him at midnight and say to him, 'Friend, lend me three loaves; for a friend of mine has come to me on his journey, and I have nothing to set before him'; and he will answer from within and say, 'Do not trouble me; the door is now shut, and my children are with me in bed; I cannot rise and give to you'? I say to you, though he will not rise and give to

him because he is his friend, yet because of his persistence he will rise and give him as many as he needs."

Now, Jesus did not intend what I am about to describe, but I have heard this passage explained as though He meant to say, *Who of you is in bed at night, when a friend comes and beats on the door until broad daylight? Finally, you stumble out of bed, and say, "Okay, if you are gonna beat on the door all night, then I'll get up and come down." So beat on God's door until you get what you want!*

This distortion suggests a picture of God as being bothered until He blesses. But persistence as Jesus taught it does not have to do with an unrelenting beating on the door in prayer until God is awakened to your need. Here's the picture He gives instead: In so many words, Jesus says, "Who of you has a friend, whose relatives unexpectedly arrive in the night? There is no food sufficient to feed them after their journey; and now they're at your door, knocking at a late hour and asking for your help. If this happened, would you say to your friend, 'Just keep beating on the door. . . . I'm really not interested in you, but I'll wait and see. If you keep pounding long enough, I might help'? Of course not!"

Jesus is teaching by contrast, showing what does *not* happen with us or with God. If a person knocks on your door at 3:00 a.m., you may not appreciate being awakened, but you are not going to get up and say, *Bug off! I don't need your wake-up call at this hour.* Instead, as the Scripture says, you will "get up and give him as many as he needs" (v. 8 WEB).

Our Savior is saying something we all need to know about God and about how He feels when we ask Him for things we need: *He doesn't mind.* It is that simple. It is the lesson Jesus means for us to hear, so we will persist in asking—continuously. Jesus presents this picture precisely to counter our human tendency toward hesitancy, to think, *My problems are too small to bother the Almighty.*

In the Greek language, "persistence" is *anaideia.* The prefix of the word, *an,* negates the related word *aidōs,* which means "modesty," "bashfulness," or "reverence." In other words, the friend's persistence in waking somebody up in the middle of the night is a kind of *un*reserve, a challenging of social propriety. The asker did not get his answer because he beat on the door until his fists were bloody but because he had the boldness to ask a friend—at night—and to directly relate a need. The nature of their relationship as friends is what emboldened him to go and say, *Hey, I need help, and I need it now!*

So Jesus is saying, *You have a Friend in heaven, and you don't need to be hesitant about asking.* You do not need to be bashful about asking or worry about being appropriately reverent. Just ask. If there is a need, get at it. Set caution aside when you approach God Almighty.

Loved one, be done with the idea that God is nervous that you might ask something outside His will and with such energy that you will force Him into something He does not really want to do. He is saying, *Be bold. Do not be afraid to ask . . . anything!*

Jesus presents a parallel concept in the parable of the persistent widow.

The Story of the Persistent Widow

Then He spoke a parable to them, that men always ought to pray and not lose heart, saying: "There was in a certain city a judge who did not fear God nor regard man. Now there was a widow in that city; and she came to him, saying, 'Get justice for me from my adversary.' And he would not for a while; but afterward he said within himself, 'Though I do not fear God nor regard man, yet because this widow troubles me

I will avenge her, lest by her continual coming she weary me.'"

Luke 18:1–5

Before we read Jesus' conclusion to this parable, let's get a clear picture of the setting:

- This was a corrupt judge.
- He did not care about God or man.
- He had no respect for either divine justice or earthly justice.
- But he still takes action in the interest of this widow because she keeps coming to him, asking that her case be handled.
- His motive is not justice for her.
- His motive (hardly noble) is that he is tired of being bothered by the woman.

Is Jesus making the judge a parallel to the Father? Obviously, no.

This is not a parable that teaches by *comparison* (as in the other story, which says, *Be bold like this*). Instead, this is a parable that teaches by *contrast*. Jesus is showing the opposite of the way things are with God.

Yet how many times I have heard otherwise? I have heard people interpret this story as though the

Bride of Christ is like the widow, a woman with a tough case who can only get God (the judge) to act by persistent complaint. But Jesus means to show God's readiness, not His reluctance. Christ's prayer message in this passage is that we should expect God to take action—and quickly.

Here is Jesus' conclusion to the lesson: "Hear what the unjust judge said. And shall God not avenge His own elect who cry out day and night to Him, though He bears long with them? I tell you that He will avenge them speedily" (Luke 18:6–8). Jesus points up the contrast between our Father in heaven—the just Judge—and a disgustingly inconsiderate, unjust human judge.

So where is the concept of persistence?

Persistence according to Jesus is *not* the desperate extension of human energy, as though we are to labor long in an attempt to see heaven disposed in our interest. Nor does He show us a God "waiting in the wings" to see if we are really sincere; and after we have squeezed blood from the bedposts in frantic prayer, He will finally say, *Okay, now that you have proven yourself sincere, I'll do something*.

That is not God's way.

Instead, *the essence of persistence is recognizing that there is no situation to which you need surrender.*

You can always ask your Friend in heaven. He will hear. You have a just Judge on your case. He will act quickly.

Yet listen, dear friend. Sometimes the answers *do* seem long in coming. And when that happens, *know* that it does not reflect heaven's disinterest.

Sometimes a long labor—a period of travail—is required before we see the birth of what we have been anticipating. But be certain: The promise will be born. What may seem long on the earthly side of things is often but a moment in glory. So have patience.

Persistence is needed, but not as a humanly energized insistence that God see our sincerity or that we try to move God to action. He does not act on the basis of our zeal; rather, He acts on the basis of our simple faith and His changeless love.

God does not need to be moved to action. He is ready *now*. But to move mountains in this world often takes a season. So wait while heaven's bulldozers are at work, and find that the mountain *is* disappearing—a truckload at a time.

And as with the birthing process, so prayer's travail often involves a time of contractions. During that season, do not give up. Hold forth boldly and praisefully to see heaven break through with new life and victory in this world.

Even if time transpires, the mountain will move. And even though hard labor may continue for a night—with tears—*joy* will come forth in the morning (see Psalm 30:5)!

f I profess with the loudest voice and clearest exposition every portion of the truth of God except precisely that little point which the world and the devil are at that moment attacking, I am not confessing Christ, however boldly I may be professing Christ. Where the battle rages, there the loyalty of the soldier is proved; and to be steady on all the battlefield besides, is mere flight and disgrace if he flinches at that point.

Martin Luther
1483–1546

Prayer That Intervenes and Reverses

He is also able to save to the uttermost those who come to God through Him, since He ever lives to make intercession for them.

Hebrews 7:25

The disciples' call to prayer is the call to a life of expanding dimensions—from worship to petition, from thanksgiving to warfare. As noted before, Ephesians 6:18 points the way to

- "praying always with all prayer" (that is, by every means of prayer)

- "and supplication" (literally, persevering for the promises, as contained in the text)
- "in the Spirit" (with supernatural assistance from Him).

Let me invite you—no, let me *urge* you—toward what lies at hand. I want to discuss three grand words that describe different ways in which we can pray: supplication, intercession and thanksgiving. But I especially want us to see them in their relationship to that order of prayer I call *the prayer that intervenes and reverses*.

Supplication

In writing to the Philippians, the apostle Paul registered one of the broadest, most inclusive and most practical calls to prayer in the Bible: "Be anxious for nothing, but in everything by prayer and supplication, with thanksgiving, let your requests be made known to God; and the peace of God, which surpasses all understanding, will guard your hearts and minds through Christ Jesus" (Philippians 4:6–7). Philippi was a Roman colony, an outpost of Rome's authority, and therefore secured with a special contingent of imperial troops.

Paul's choice of terms, noting the *promise* of prayer, takes on special meaning in this light. When he says, "The peace of God . . . will guard your hearts and minds," he uses the Greek word for "guard"—the garrisoning of Roman troops to secure a colony. In other words, he was saying, *If you will take a specific stance in prayer, God will establish a stronghold in your mind, bracing you against the adversary so that you will never be cast into tumult or confusion, whatever your trial or need.*

This text points the way for our entry into this place of secured confidence following prayer. But it involves more than simple petition—ordinary, give-us-this-day-our-daily-bread asking. Paul calls us to "supplication," an interesting word in the Greek language (*deomai*) that essentially has to do with "asking" but extends the idea further.

Strong's Concordance has linked in alphabetical sequence the words *dei, deomai* and *deō*. When I looked up the first, my discovery of these words in their natural *lexical* order helped me to see them in their *logical* order. First, their definitions:

- *Deomai*: "to supplicate or to make supplication," "to beg" or "to pray earnestly"
- *Deō*: "to bind something up" or "to tie something up"

- *Dei*: "ought" or "it is necessary" (a Greek particle used to express the moral imperative)

The "moral imperative" refers to that which in the order of things "ought" to be. For example, if there is a need, we *ought* to help. If there is a fire, we *ought* to do something—help, warn someone, get water or even put it out. "Ought" means, in the order of things, to do what is necessary and right.

Now, it was seemingly by accident that in discovering the linguistic relationship of these words, I began to grasp the concept of supplication (that is, the pivotal difference between simply asking and supplicating): To ask is to simply make our request known, and we have dealt with that already. But supplication answers to those times when a focused point of *passion* in prayer is needed. And when this need is joined to our recognition of the privileges we have been given in prayer, a distinct dimension of prayer emerges.

I had always been puzzled by *deomai* being translated "to beg" where prayer was involved, since Jesus does not *ever* teach prayer as begging. It does not reflect our relationship with God. But when we look at the cognate, *deō* ("to bind"), the dynamic between prayer and spiritual authority comes clearly into view.

Consider Jesus' teaching regarding the authority His Church shall be given over the dark powers of hell: "And I will give you the keys of the kingdom of heaven, and whatever you bind on earth will be bound in heaven, and whatever you loose on earth will be loosed in heaven" (Matthew 16:19). Based on that quote, it appears that *deomai*, as a prayer exercise called supplication, implies more than earnest begging. The evidence is that we are to see supplication as involving the Christ-authorized action of binding up certain things.

Understandably then, we ask, What things do I have the *right* to bind up? The answer, I believe, is in our seeing the cognate relationship of *dei* to *deomai*. It would seem we are assigned to bind up things that are *not* what they ought to be and see them through in prayer until they *are* what they ought to be. Supplication, thus seen, is prayer that can return things to their intended order—to what is proper or ought to be.

Look at our world, created under a divine order now long since violated. We understand that so much of our world is as it is because the order God intended has fallen into confusion, chaos and disarray due to the Fall, human sin, and satanic activity. Now, seeing things "out of order," God has ordained a *Mission: Possible* for we who have come under *His* order. We not only have the privilege of *fellowship* in prayer but also an invitation to *partnership* in prayer—to learn a dimension of binding by prayer unto the reconstitution of His original order and intent for peoples' lives and circumstances.

Supplication moves into the confusion of the fallen order of things (for example, a broken heart, a broken home, someone's broken health) and begins through supplication to bind up broken things, drawing the strands of such binding back to what ought to be according to God's intent and God's will.

In short, the praying Church has been empowered by Christ's promise to pray in ways that stop the plans that hell's councils are trying to advance. This is what is meant by prayers that bind and loose. Binding is not limited to how we may conceive of something being tied up; it is also based on the concept of binding as it is used when a contract has been made.

For example, when a property is being developed, an architect will regularly visit the site, meeting with the contractor to assure the details of the contract are fulfilled. Holding the contractor to the contract is legally possible because the terms of a contract are binding—but possible only as the architect or his representative insists on the "binding" clauses of the contract, ensuring that contested or neglected features of the project will be finished as they ought to be and as the owner wills.

The analogy is obvious. In this world, Satan is trying to construct things that are totally out of line from God's blueprint. You and I are on-site observers of what is taking place in human lives and earthly circumstances that come to our awareness. When what ought to be is not, our role in supplication is to say:

Lord, what You contracted for at the cross, for Your purpose and power to save [name] or deliver [name], isn't being done on earth. Let Your ruling power, Your kingdom, come! Let Your will be done on earth as it is in heaven. Lord, as Your agent assigned to this case in prayer, I say stop the adversary's advance. According to Calvary's terms, I "bind" the enemy from success. According to Your will through the power of Jesus' blood, I loose on earth what You have already willed in heaven.

Please notice that the grammar of the Greek phrase, translated in essence "whatever you bind will be bound, whatever you loose will be loosed," makes one thing clear that sometimes goes unnoted. It is important that we understand this fact:

Our binding only accomplishes on earth what has *already been* accomplished in heaven.

In other words, we do not *make* things happen; prayer *releases* their happening. God has ordained the intended order, so we are not creators of what occurs but rather *releasers* of what He has desired to be, but which our flesh or the devil oppose. So when we bind or loose, remember, His is the power and the provision; ours is the privilege of participation. Further, may we always be wise and praiseful, knowing the source of the power we exercise. Where does it flow from?

The cross!

Never forget it, loved one. Jesus' death on the cross broke the adversary's rule over us once and forever. Apart from Calvary's power, we are no different. You and I have no defense in our own power. We are all helpless against Satan's strategies or contrivances, *except* that when we have the resources of Calvary, we not only have a sure defense for our own soul but also a point of appeal in calling for heaven's best in the face of hell's worst.

Because of Jesus' victory through the blood of His cross, prayers of supplication can bind—we can contract for heaven's ought-to-be deliverance and rejoice in seeing God's will done.

In this light, then, it is not surprising that Paul said when we pray that way, the peace of God will guard our hearts. Prayer (asking) and supplication (binding and loosing) lay the groundwork for a deep peace to possess the soul if, as Philippians 4:6 says, praises of thanksgiving are offered with them. Faith brings peace, and anxiety will cease.

Prayer has found a place of confidence by calling on heaven's resource and victory and by applying them in simple faith. Then with thanksgiving, we rest in praise as heaven's power moves to actuate the holy will and purpose of God's intended order on earth as in heaven. Our prayers are set forward in Calvary's power of release, for God's glory and in Jesus' name. Amen.

Intercession

Continuing with "all prayer" as our goal, let's look at the idea of intercession. Considering the apostle Paul's admonition in 1 Timothy 2:1–3, it is important and impressive to see the priority this order of prayer is given along with supplication:

> Therefore I exhort first of all that supplications, prayers, intercessions, and giving of thanks be made for all men, for kings and all who are in

authority, that we may lead a quiet and peaceable life in all godliness and reverence. For this is good and acceptable in the sight of God our Savior.

Of particular significance are the *place* and the *scope* indicated—the priority ("first of all") and the aegis of influence ("for kings and all who are in authority").

In this foundational New Testament call to intercession, we have what I believe is the Bible's fundamental realm of assignment with regard to civic and political affairs. The directive is to pray for civic issues that are grander and broader than our own immediate points of personal concern or involvement. Obedience to this call will disallow any notion or practice of prayer as a preoccupying, self-centered concern. We are promised influence that can affect the climate of a culture ("that we may lead a quiet and peaceable life").

Understandably, it would be tempting to say, *Who am I to suppose that when I kneel, I can decide the moral, spiritual, political, military or economic circumstances in my country? In my world?* But the Word of God not only says intercession has that capacity; it also specifically says intercession is one of our *first* assignments—a priority which, if observed, can reveal the living Church's real role in determining government. (While I believe Christians in a free society should vote and be as politically active or involved as they feel called, the Bible says little about direct political control. Yet it has *much* to say about the intercessor's role in praying for governments.)

"Effective" and "Fervent" Prayer in James

In James 5:16, the Bible notes, "The effective, fervent prayer of a righteous man avails much." The text, freely translated, reads, "The spiritually energized prayer of an impassioned person seeking God will count for more than he or she can imagine. Look how!" Then the prophet Elijah is mentioned as an illustration of such prayer:

> Elijah was a man with a nature like ours, and he prayed earnestly that it would not rain; and it did not rain on the land for three years and six months. And he prayed again, and the heaven gave rain, and the earth produced its fruit.

> vv. 17–18

A study of the Old Testament text being referenced here (1 Kings 17:1; 18:1–46) reveals a dramatic story of social, spiritual, economic and, yes, meteorological impact through one man's intercession. The climate of the culture was *literally* changed, as drought conditions gave way to life-giving rain. The same passage shows Elijah's victory over the prophets of Baal—a spiritual triumph—and the breaking of a drought, which would have had obvious economic and social impact. God's judgment on the people was reversed, and this magnificent passage in James says that same potential is available today.

The broad, sweeping possibilities of intercession are unfolded in an examination of the Greek and Hebrew words used to indicate this type of prayer. *Entynchanō* (Greek) and *paga* (Hebrew) have essentially the same meaning—a definition that seems peculiar to most when first heard. Both mean to "light upon," "come upon by accident" or "strike" (as lightning, unpredictably).

The Word Paga in the Old Testament

Maybe you are like me, and your first exposure to those definitions evoked a bit of bewilderment. *Prayer by accident?* Let me give some examples of the use of *paga* in the Old Testament to demonstrate the awesome truth in this word.

In Genesis 28, Jacob is seen in flight, running from his brother, Esau. He comes to a place that will eventually be named Bethel. As he arrives there, he looks for a place to rest. During the night of sleep, he had the vision known as Jacob's ladder. When he awakened the next morning—after God met him in a dynamically powerful way, giving him a promise for his whole future—Jacob says, "Surely the LORD is in this place, and I did not know it" (v. 16). The day before, however, when he stopped at that site, Scripture says, "He lighted upon a certain place" (v. 11 KJV).

In other words, to Jacob's eye this was a random place of stopping; but in God's plan, it would become the milestone of his life. Therein lies the idea of intercession. What seems random—catching us unexpectedly in time and circumstance and commanding our attention—is not accidental but *providential*.

Dear one, almost every day of our lives, you and I step into apparently random situations. If we perceive they are ordained of the Spirit, we will learn to respond to them, knowing God has brought us to them. There will be occasions when we will have a seemingly random thought, or a "signaling," which might seem accidental; but wisdom will teach us to seize these moments as intended by God to cause us to intercede for someone or some situation.

The issue of intercession does not have to do only with grand national and international issues, as we have already reflected upon, but also with anything that the Lord places before us as a point intersecting our daily lives. Perhaps you are driving along and see an accident in the roadway. Recognize that in God's providence, He has you present to intercede.

Please capture the divine significance of this for a moment. In many cases, you and I are the only people He has on the scene who have sufficient spiritual sensitivity to know that we can make a difference. The Lord wants to salt all of society with people who have this understanding—people who recognize that, as intercessors, they are present for the purpose of travailing in prayer for a world that otherwise would experience only the tragic consequences of life's problems, without the hope of divine entry to their circumstance through intercession.

Intercession occurs when people realize God has ordained boundaries of blessing for human experiences, and unless someone prays, Satan will try to violate the boundary line. He will try to make the experience less than it would have been in God's counsel and covenant. Intercession sees that God's purposes reach all the way unto what He wills.

Unfortunately, many of God's people have adopted a mind-set of passivity, a kind of spiritual sloth that causes us to think, *Well, God is all-powerful. He can do whatever He wants, and I'll sort of agree to it. Isn't that what "Thy kingdom come, Thy will be done" means?* (Matthew 6:10 KJV).

No, dear one.

Jesus taught us to pray, "Thy kingdom come, Thy will be done" on this earthly side of things. We, the redeemed troops, therefore, must fight the good fight and see heaven's covenant established and extended in the name of the King. We are not praying, *Oh well, I guess, "Thy kingdom come, and Thy will be done."* Instead, we are praying, *I stand as heaven's ambassador on this planet. And I say, "God's kingdom come here, in this setting, and God's will be done."*

Intercession is insisting on the extension of heaven's covenanted boundaries, which hell will encroach upon and try to push back to less than what God has intended. We are the ones appointed to monitor the situation. In prayer we represent heaven's *purposes*, by heaven's *power*, speaking heaven's *covenant* into the situation; and we watch God actuate it according to our calling upon Him.

The word *paga* is also found in 1 Samuel 22. During the time of his backsliding as king of Israel, Saul was offended by some of the priests. He ordered his own troops to fall on them and kill them, but his troops respected God's priests too much to obey their own king. It was an embarrassment to him, so Saul turned to a pagan man, Doeg the Edomite, who had joined his entourage, and said, "Turn thou, and fall upon the priests" (v. 18 KJV). The hateful Edomite seized the moment, grabbed a sword and began to lop off the heads of God's priests. The Bible says that Doeg turned and "fell upon [*paga*] the priests" (v. 18 KJV).

Now, I admit that the scene, the slaying of God's priests, is tragic. But the verb, objectively used in this setting, represents a person who goes on the attack, falling upon the perceived adversary of his king. It is a lesson in intercession, except in our case, our adversary is the devil, who "walks about like a roaring lion, seeking whom he may devour" (1 Peter 5:8). In intercessory prayer, you and I are taking the sword of the Spirit and, at the direction of our King, falling upon the adversary, cutting off his efforts to attack and stopping his advance.

Intercession is such a dynamic form of prayer. It involves our ensuring on earth the boundaries of God's heavenly purposes, defending against the enemy's encroachment, recognizing our privilege to take action at apparently random encounters and *controlling the climate* of societies and nations.

The Role of Intercessor in Romans

So how do we exercise the role of intercessor? In Romans 8:26–27, we read how the Holy Spirit is available to help us in this prayer dimension:

> Likewise the Spirit also helps in our weaknesses. For we do not know what we should pray for as we ought, but the Spirit Himself makes intercession for us with groanings which cannot be uttered. Now He who searches the hearts knows what the mind of the Spirit is, because He makes intercession for the saints according to the will of God.

Note the proximity of these two verses to the oft quoted verse that follows: "And we know that all things work together for good to those who love God, to those who are the called according to His purpose" (v. 28).

This much-loved verse must never be removed from its context. Romans 8:26–28 needs to be considered as a whole, for it shows how when intercession is energized by the Holy Spirit are brought to bear upon situations we do not understand, *then* there comes the entry of God's purpose—at which point "all things work together for good."

Listen to me, dear one: All things *do not* work together for good in this world—not automatically.

Nothing works together for good in this world on its own. But intercession is the pivot point determining *if* God's good will penetrate all things. As that occurs, and we partner with Him in understanding and undertaking our prayer role, we allow the likeness of His Son to be developed in us.

Jesus' likeness is not only one of character; it is also one of spiritual authority. Jesus not only walked in purity of conduct, but He also walked about setting straight things that had been corrupted by the works of darkness. Remember Acts 10:38: "How God anointed Jesus of Nazareth . . . who went about doing good and healing all who were oppressed by the devil." Jesus was not just a good man. He was *God's* man.

So as the Lord calls us to be conformed to the image of Christ (see Romans 8:29), learning Holy Spirit–assisted intercession is a part of our character growth in Christ—a part of being conformed to His image as disciples.

Thanksgiving

Finally, learn the power of thanksgiving, which Paul describes in one of his letters to the believers in Thessalonica: "Rejoice always, pray without ceasing, in everything give thanks; for this is the will of God in Christ Jesus for you" (1 Thessalonians 5:16–18).

The Bible does not say everything is a thank-worthy thing. It says, in everything you *see*, be thankful. For example, if you saw the flames of a small brush fire threatening your home, you would not stand there and say, *Thank God!* Instead, you would grab a rug to beat the fire out or spray water to drench it. But when hell's fire begins to draw near through tough or painful circumstance, the Bible says to use praise and thanksgiving—to God for His almightiness—to strike down the blaze.

We are not told to give thanks *for* everything but rather *in* everything. That is, in the middle of everything, however desperate, *give thanks*.

How? Go out and begin slapping down hell's flames with praise to God. Shout to the high heavens that God is able to master this situation by His dominion, which you welcome with your worship. Say:

- *I thank God this situation can't master us.*
- *I thank God He is bigger than what is happening right now.*
- *I thank God that though I had this accident, He is going to move into this scene and assist me.*

- *I thank God that though my sister has been diagnosed with cancer, we have a living Lord who is going to sustain us.*
- *I thank God that though I seem to be weak in my body today, He has promised me His strength and resources.*

In everything, give thanks!

This is what Paul is saying when he writes, "For this is the will of God" (v. 18). Are cancer, difficulties and accidents the will of God? No. But the *spirit of thanksgiving* is the will of God concerning you.

As we look at worship, petition, supplication, intercession and thanksgiving, we are seeing some of the exceeding wonders of prayer for application in our personal lives, as we live in the power of the Spirit as growing disciples of Christ.

But lo' the snare is broke, the captive's
    freed,
By faith on all the hostile powers we tread,
And crush through Jesus' strength the Ser-
    pent's head.
Jesus hath cast the cursed Accuser down,
Hath rooted up the tares by Satan sown:
All nature bows to His benign command,
And two are one in His almighty hand.

Charles Wesley
1707–1788

The Practice of Fasting

As they ministered to the Lord and fasted,
the Holy Spirit said, "Now separate to Me
Barnabas and Saul for the work to which I
have called them." Then, having fasted and
prayed, and laid hands on them, they sent
them away.

Acts 13:2–3

We should not leave the subject of the exceeding wonders of prayer without dealing with
the remarkable power of prayer joined to fasting (abstinence from food for a certain amount of time).
Fasting as a discipline is not meant to simply demand
obedience of my body by submitting to this affliction

of no food. Rather, it should be done as an active response to the revelation of the Scriptures on the subject. But when we deal with the subject of fasting, we encounter a couple of unusual problems.

First, believers can become confused regarding fasting, as though it were done to generate an energy born of our own exercise, as though fasting were a means of earning something from God. But the dedication and devotion involved in any exercise of prayer, including fasting, never has anything to do with our *getting* from God or "forcing" God into action. Rather, prayer and fasting are means of aligning ourselves with His possibilities of power through applying His principles of obedience in order to participate in His promises.

Second, for some people, the problematic question arises as to whether fasting is even relevant, necessary or important today. Some have suggested that it is not, relegating fasting to the realm of the archaic, as though it is some medieval form of legalistic church tradition—people doing penance in an effort to purge themselves before God's eyes by punishing their bodies through abstaining from food.

But notwithstanding these points of misunderstanding, the Bible speaks very clearly and pointedly about fasting being a part of a Christian disciple's practice. Hear it from Jesus' own lips:

Then the disciples of John came to Him, saying, "Why do we and the Pharisees fast often, but Your disciples do not fast?"

And Jesus said to them, "Can the friends of the bridegroom mourn as long as the bridegroom is with them? But the days will come when the bridegroom will be taken away from them, and then they will fast."

Matthew 9:14–15

By this Jesus means, *As long as I'm here, this isn't the time for fasting, but when I am gone . . . yes.* He is referring here to the season from His ascension until He returns again. Thus, in plain words, Jesus not only *allows*, but seems to *appoint* fasting as a Christian discipline.

Further, Paul enunciates fasting as a vital part of the life of a servant of Christ. In describing his own practices "in fastings often" (2 Corinthians 11:27), he verifies two things: (1) He made frequent application of fasting, and (2) he did not fast according to a calendar. He conveys the *rightness* of the discipline without a requirement of *ritual*. In short, the Holy Spirit can and will direct us to times of fasting.

The Bible shows fasting as having played a powerful role in some very dramatic and dynamic situations. The fact that many of these are Old Testament examples should not in any way discourage our taking them seriously for today: "For whatever things were written before were written for our learning, that we through the patience and comfort of the Scriptures might have hope" (Romans 15:4).

Clearly, we are told in the New Testament that Old Testament principles are for our instruction, and we are wise to observe those that apply to our lives as Jesus' disciples. Let's look at four examples in the Old Testament in which the faithful fasted in situations similar to our circumstances today.

Four Lessons Taught for Today

> And they mourned and wept and fasted until evening for Saul and for Jonathan his son, for the people of the LORD and for the house of Israel, because they had fallen by the sword.
>
> 2 Samuel 1:12

Fasting at Transition

Saul and Jonathan had been slain. Because Israel had lost her leader and heir to the throne, David exercises a time of fasting and seeking the

Lord. David eventually became ruler over all the tribes of Israel. The significance?

Consider the wisdom of people humbling themselves in the face of a successful attack by their adversary. Then consider the way you could apply a fast at a personal level or group dimension when destructive events assail your life. As you do, seek the Lord and expect the same result to be manifest—only now it will be the *Son of David* who will rise to rule over your circumstance.

Fasting for Survival

In Esther 4:16, the queen called her own people to fast. In essence, Esther tells Mordecai, "Go to the Jewish community and tell them to fast, and I'll go before the king and plead their case." The story is a crucial one in Jewish history. The life of the nation was on the line. As we study the flow of human history, we understand that such moments are more than merely political affairs; they are deadly satanic attacks, as are any efforts to destroy an entire people.

Here Esther takes her place in fasting and her posture in intercession. As she goes before the king, behind her approach was a people who were fasting and seeking God. Similarly, there are times when we face situations where seemingly everything is at stake. But by seeking the Lord with fasting and intercessory supplication, we can discover His way to reverse the situation and see God's rule and grace enter in.

Fasting for the Future

Read Ezra 8:21–23 and see how great projects are best undertaken by the preparation of fasting and prayer.

The exiled Jews were preparing to return to Jerusalem with a large contingent of families and their valuables, including precious implements for reinstating worship in the Temple. Ezra, their leader, says something along the lines of, "I didn't have the nerve to go to the rulers who were releasing us and ask for soldiers to accompany and protect us on our journey." He knew the pagan onlookers were already marveling at how God was working on his people's behalf (see Psalm 126:1–3); to request human protection would seem to suggest that God could not do the job.

But Ezra does do something: He calls the people to fast, "that we might humble ourselves before our God, to seek from Him the right way for us and our little ones and all our possessions" (Ezra

8:21). Listen to it! There is something tender in these words, as a man describes a people seeking God's protection for, and guidance into, the future. They were fasting to make the transition to where God was taking them.

Sound familiar? Are you seeking a new time in your life? Are you looking for God's protection and leading as you navigate a present opportunity? Seek Him with fasting and prayer. And remember, Ezra focused not only on today's need but also on the way this action would serve future generations—our little ones.

Fasting and Spiritual Warfare

The Lord had revealed to Daniel great prophetic promises, grand disclosures of His purposes, but they were a long time in coming about: "The message was true, but the appointed time was long" (Daniel 10:1). The prophecy was not coming to full realization, so Daniel begins to seek God with fasting and prayer.

Please notice that fasting is not something that is exercised apart from impassioned prayer. We have spoken about supplication, intercession, thanksgiving, petition and worship. You will discover that most of these practices are evident in Daniel's prayer in 9:1–19. It is an extensive, intensive prayer—but notice also it is joined to a fast.

Fasting and prayer go together. Fasting without prayer is simply going without food. It is not "foodlessness" but prayer—seeking God—that makes fasting powerful. We are not on a hunger strike, protesting God's inactivity. Dark spiritual powers are resisted and broken through fasting. As Daniel sought the Lord, God's purpose was released, and a prophetic promise fulfilled—the prophetic promise of the termination of Israel's exile in Babylonia.

Can you imagine how many situations today are awaiting someone who will recognize that God's time for deliverance has come? How many people "exiled from God's purpose" might be released as *we* fast and pray unto that objective?

"Nothing but Prayer and Fasting"

> So He said to them, "This kind can come out by nothing but prayer and fasting."
>
> Mark 9:29

When Jesus returned with Peter, James and John from the Mount of Transfiguration, He found the other disciples frustrated with their unsuccessful efforts to cast out a demon from a local boy. They asked Him, "Why could we not cast it out?" (Mark 9:28). In verse 29, Jesus is speaking to His disciples about a circumstance they had found themselves incapable of handling.

Please note this text in your Bible, because I regret to tell you that some contemporary translations do not contain the whole verse. Some scholars have judged it to be insufficiently supported by manuscript evidence to retain it. Nevertheless, there is virtually as much manuscript evidence to support the phrase "and fasting" as to omit it.

In *The Expositor's Greek Testament*, Dr. O. Morrison notes: "The authorization for omitting 'and fasting' with prayer because of its absence in some ancient manuscripts, really is not sufficient. But even if it were overwhelmingly so, fasting would in its essence be implied in this text."* In other words, "and fasting" should not be omitted, but in any case, fasting is at the very least implied. I press this point because I fear some may feel that its omission in some translations suggests fasting is not important, even though Jesus said His disciples would exercise fasting as an abiding discipline until He comes again.

---

*W. R. Nicoll, ed., *The Expositor's Greek Testament* (George H. Doran Company: New York, 1897), 404.

It is important that we recognize the power of fasting for breaking yokes of spiritual darkness. Remember, fasting is not about *earning* things from God but is for *learning* things from Him. And specifically, through fasting we can learn a realm of spiritual authority over the adversary, which we will not be able to explain until we are on the heaven side of things. But Jesus does make it clear that fasting—with prayer—holds a dynamic that breaks evil power: "This kind only comes out this way!" (see Mark 9:29).

I do not know why, but somehow while I seek God, fasting drains hellish powers of their capacity to withstand the entry of God's Kingdom. Jesus has said it, and that settles it. So let's learn from this event—and the other pivotal and practical illustrations the Scriptures give—of the power of fasting as a discipline.

Practical Guidelines

In our congregation's life, many of us choose to fast for at least two meals every Wednesday. According to Wesleyan tradition, John Wesley and his followers fasted every Wednesday and Friday, from morning until afternoon tea at four o'clock. Other churches encourage seasons of fasting, and I do not mean to devalue their observance or think them unwise. But I do not consider those who choose not to fast to be failed Christians.

Nevertheless, the discipline begs the question, "When might I fast?"

Here are a few words of counsel on how to observe the fast: Simply stated, to begin it requires just plain good sense. And as I have already said, it involves frequent prayer. But people often ask other very practical questions—for example, "How long shall I fast?"

Only the Holy Spirit can direct you regarding the length of your fast, but practical considerations ought to be kept in view. Begin by asking the Lord to lead you as to how long your fast should continue. Some people's work requires such a heavy energy expenditure that it may not allow for a total fast.

Remember, Jesus' forty-day fast was not carried on while He was keeping office hours or working at the plant every day. He went into the wilderness and was completely away from it all during that season of fasting. A day's fast as a regular discipline is the practice of many. Also, the three-day "believer's fast" has a long history in the Church.

When Daniel went on his 21-day fast, the Bible says he took "no pleasant food" (Daniel 10:3). The concept is that he did not satisfy his appetite; he ate only enough to sustain himself. This was a voluntary reduction of intake, denying himself delicacies yet still answering the basic need for energy. This is an acceptable fast—observed with a perfect spirit.

Further, because we are not trying to convince God of our worthiness but rather are simply observing a biblically taught discipline, it is not unspiritual to recognize there will be functional and practical considerations at the physical level and they ought to be understood. Here are a few.

First, do not fast if there are medical or dietary reasons that prohibit it. One of my dearest mentors, my first bishop and my lifelong friend, Dr. Vincent Bird, had diabetes; yet before he went to be with the Lord, He said to me a number of times, "When the congregation fasts, I've learned how to be in the *spirit* of a fast." By this he meant that he applied it with his heart, seeking God in a special way that only he could describe. As a diabetic, he obviously needed to keep eating, but he still moved into the ministry of prayer with a special spirit—in power, but also in practical wisdom. Never be so foolish as to violate medically directed dietary requirements and then claim that some spiritual pursuit brought you to such folly.

Second, understand that your body needs water. As a normal requirement, you should drink at least eight glasses of water daily—especially during a fast. Water is not a violation of your fast. When Jesus fasted the forty days, the Bible says that "in those days He ate nothing" (Luke 4:2). This specific mention indicates no abstinence from fluids. So, keep in mind, even our miracle-working Savior needed water. (Incidentally, some of the most spiritual people I know have suggested to me that a squeeze of lemon in the water when fasting is helpful. It helps the body to cast off impurities during the fast, assisting the body's cleansing.)

Third, some individuals, whose regimen cannot tolerate a complete fast, may find that drinking fruit juice will help them to remain in the spirit of the fast. I am not suggesting this procedure as an escape if the Lord calls you to a more complete fast; rather, recognize this as one way to diminish your food intake during an appropriate pursuit of a fast. And in this vein, those who for some reason may be unable to participate at all, but whose partner is fasting, can still sustain a partnership in the fast by giving themselves to regular times of prayer beyond their usual pattern. No condemnation should be felt by one for not fasting along with one's spouse or prayer partner.

Fourth, fasting should be joined to special times of prayer, praise and intercession. For example, during a fasting time, why not set five-minute prayer breaks each hour or devote an entire lunchtime to prayer and praise. Seek out brothers and sisters in Christ who will feel a partnership with your seeking God in such a fashion, but only if they feel it is their desire and not the imposition of some religious pushiness on your part.

Finally, spend extra time in the Word of God when fasting. The psalmist wrote, "Your word is a lamp to my feet and a light to my path," and David said, "The judgments of the LORD . . . are sweeter . . . than the honeycomb" (Psalms 119:105; 19:9–10). Jesus said the Word of God is nourishment to the soul (see Matthew 4:4). So feed on it.

And as you fast, be further nourished in knowing the pleasure of obedience to God: "My food is to do the will of Him who sent Me" (John 4:34). Those simple words spoken by Jesus express a concept of nourishment that we can partake of, especially in times of fasting, as we seek the release of the power that comes through this basic Christian discipline joined with prayer.

I was also led into a state of great dissatisfaction with my own want of stability in faith and love. . . . I often felt myself weak in the presence of temptation and needed frequently to hold days of fasting and prayer . . . that would enable me efficiently to labor.

Charles G. Finney
1792–1875

Personal Prayer Journal

Personal Prayer Journal

Personal Prayer Journal

Personal Prayer Journal

Jack W. Hayford is founding pastor and pastor emeritus of The Church On The Way in Van Nuys, California, and chancellor emeritus of The King's University in Dallas (Gateway Church). He is also founder of the Jack W. Hayford School of Pastoral Nurture—a ministry that has impacted thousands of pastors from more than fifty denominations and numerous independent groups. In travels, he has spoken to more than twenty thousand church leaders annually and has ministered in more than fifty nations.

Jack has also written more than fifty books and composed nearly six hundred hymns and choruses, including the internationally known "Majesty." His radio and television ministry has extended throughout the United States and into most parts of the world. He has served on numerous boards of Christian ministries and agencies, including from 2005 to 2009 as president of the denomination in which he has pastored since his licensing (1956) and ordination (1960).

Jack is a graduate of LIFE Bible College in Los Angeles and Azusa Pacific University (also located in Southern California). In 1998, APU designated him as the university's Alumnus of the Year.

Additional information may be obtained by contacting:

The King's University
2121 E. Southlake Blvd.
Southlake, TX 76092

or

gateway.kingsuniversity.edu
jackhayford.org

More Wisdom from Jack Hayford!

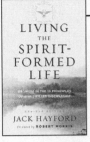

In our busy, distraction-prone lives, we often overlook the rich, fulfilling work of tending our souls—discovering deeper meaning and lasting satisfaction.

In what has become a modern-day classic, bestselling author and beloved pastor Jack Hayford shows how we can feed our deepest places in the midst of our fast-paced culture. With warmth and wisdom he reveals how we can link our souls to timeless practices and principles set forth in Scripture, and he invites you to rediscover the power and blessing of these Spirit-filled disciplines. Even more, Pastor Jack shows how these spiritual disciplines are relevant for today and how we can practice them in the here and now.

Living the Spirit-Formed Life